Contents

Be considerate!

When visiting a place of worship, remember that it is sacred to believers and so be considerate to their feelings. It doesn't take a lot of effort – just attitude.

A member of a choir sings hymns

What does a church look like?

There are many different kinds of churches. Each church looks different, but they all have some things in common.

A church is a place where Christians gather together to worship God.

A church is not the only place where Christians worship, but because churches are the most common religious buildings in the United Kingdom, there is probably one very close to where you live.

▼ (1) This is a church that was built in Saxon times – over a 1,000 years ago. Notice how small it is and especially how small the windows are.

▼ (2) Many country churches were built during a period of time called the Middle Ages, which happened between 1,000 and 500 years ago. The oldest part of this church is on the right. An extension was built on the left in Victorian times (just over a 100 years ago).

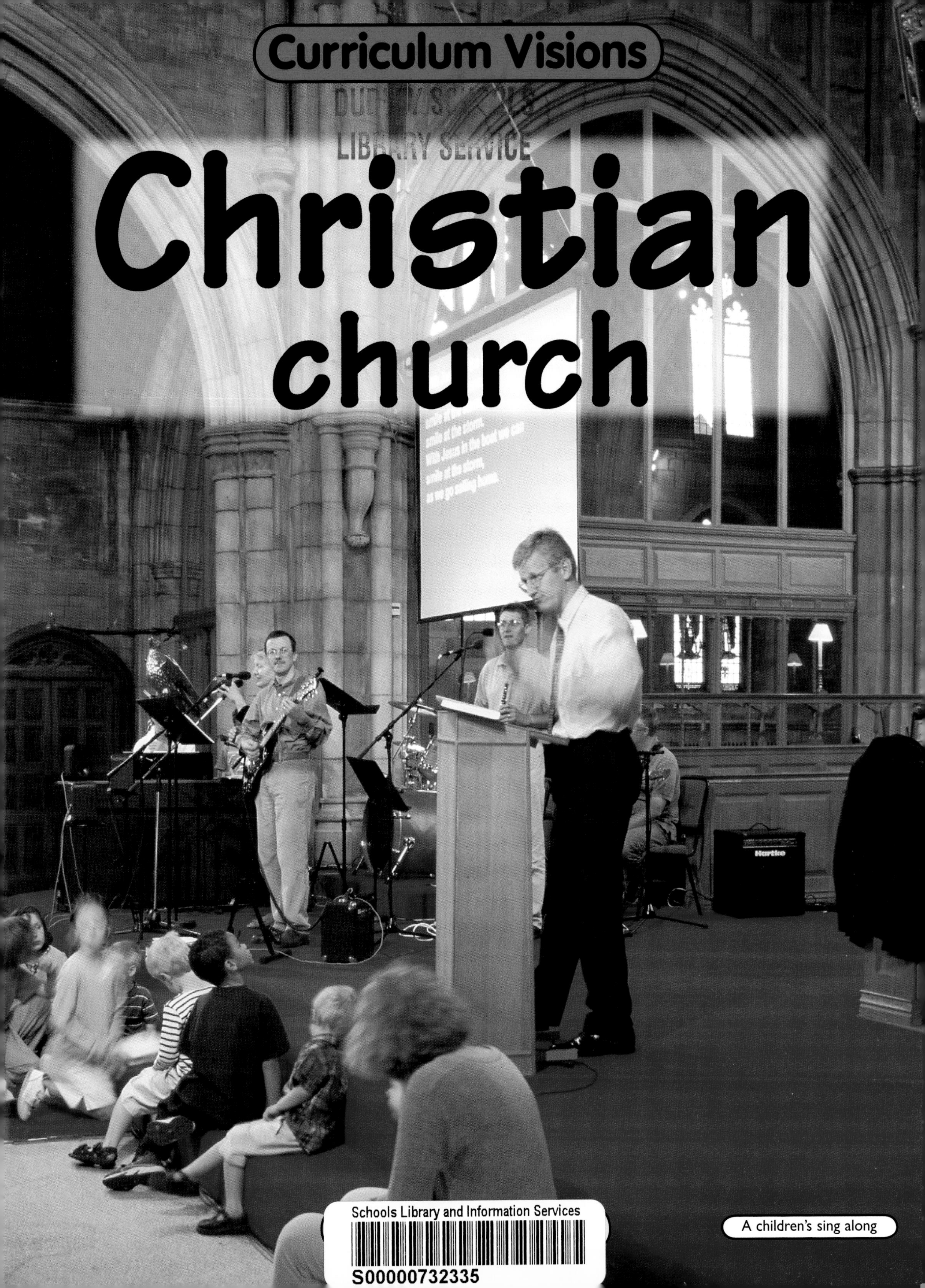
Curriculum Visions
Christian
church
smile at the storm,
With Jesus in the boat we can
smile at the storm,
as we go sailing home.
Hartke
A children's sing along

Word list

Look out for these words as you go through the book. They are shown using CAPITALS.

ALTAR The main focus of worship in a church. The altar is sometimes carved from stone or made of wood. It can also be a simple table. The altar has a flat top and might have objects on it, such as a cross and a Bible.

BAPTISE/BAPTISM A ceremony where a person is sprinkled with water, or immersed in water, as a way of showing they are a Christian.

BAPTISTRY A large container for water. In some churches, adults are baptised by getting into a baptistry and putting their whole body under the water.

BIBLE The book containing the main teachings of Christianity.

CATHEDRAL The most important or mother church of a diocese.

CHALICE A cup that is used to hold wine during the Eucharist ceremony. The chalice can be plain or decorated.

CHANCEL The eastern part of a church and the place between the nave and the altar.

CHAPEL A small, or medium-sized room in a Roman Catholic or Anglican church that is used for private worship or by a small group of worshippers. A Methodist church building is also called a chapel.

CLERGY, MEMBER OF THE CLERGY A person who has been specially trained to lead worship.

CONFESSIONAL Some Christians believe that it is important to confess their sins to God while a priest listens. This is done in private, in a small room or a curtained-off area called a confessional.

CONGREGATION All the people who are worshipping at a service.

CRUCIFY/CRUCIFIXION Jesus was killed when he was nailed (at his wrists and ankles) to a large, wooden cross. This is called crucifixion.

CRYPT An underground chamber where sometimes people are buried in a church.

DIOCESE An important area for the Roman Catholic and Anglican churches. It is overseen by a bishop.

DISCIPLE One of the first 12 followers of Jesus Christ.

EUCHARIST, HOLY COMMUNION, LORD'S SUPPER, MASS A ceremony where Christians drink a small amount of wine and eat a piece of special bread in order to remember Jesus' last supper with his disciples.

FONT A large container filled with water that has been blessed. The font is usually on a stand.

JESUS CHRIST The founder of Christianity. He died in 33 AD.

NAVE The main part of the church. The nave often looks like a big hall.

ORDINATION When someone who has been training to be a priest is given permission to lead acts of worship. The ceremony is led by the bishop.

PEWS Long benches where people sit during services.

PULPIT A raised position where a person stands to give the sermon.

REMEMBRANCE/VOTIVE CANDLES Candles which are sometimes lit in order to help remember other people or people who have died.

SCREEN A large painted board or cloth used to separate different parts of the church.

SERMON Teaching or preaching during a service.

SERVICE Religious worship. A service might include prayer, songs, a sermon and readings from the Bible.

SPIRE A pointed church tower.

STAINED GLASS Coloured or painted glass.

STATIONS OF THE CROSS Many churches have 14 plaques or paintings on the wall that show 14 things that are believed to have happened to Jesus on his way to be crucified. These plaques are called the stations of the cross.

TABERNACLE (AUMBRY) The bread used in the Eucharist is sometimes kept in a special cupboard called the Tabernacle.

TOWER A tall structure. In churches the tower often has bells inside.

VIRGIN MARY The mother of Jesus Christ.

▲ ③ **Many city churches have been built in recent years, to cater for the needs of growing numbers of city dwellers.**

They have most of the same features as older churches, such as a cross and a bell tower.

What churches have in common

You may be familiar with your own local church, but do you know what most churches have in common? Here are some pictures of churches to help you (pictures ①, ②, ③ and ④).

Let's begin by imagining ourselves outside a church. What would we see? In most cases we would see a tall building with large windows and **STAINED GLASS**. All but the oldest churches on this page look like this.

Towers, spires and bells

Most churches have a **TOWER**, a **SPIRE** or simply a single bell above the roof.

Just as in other religions, in the days before people had clocks and wristwatches, the bells were rung to remind people when it was time for the **SERVICE**. Bells are still rung, however, as part of Christian tradition.

▼ ④ **This is a modern city church built in new suburbs. It is only a few years old.**

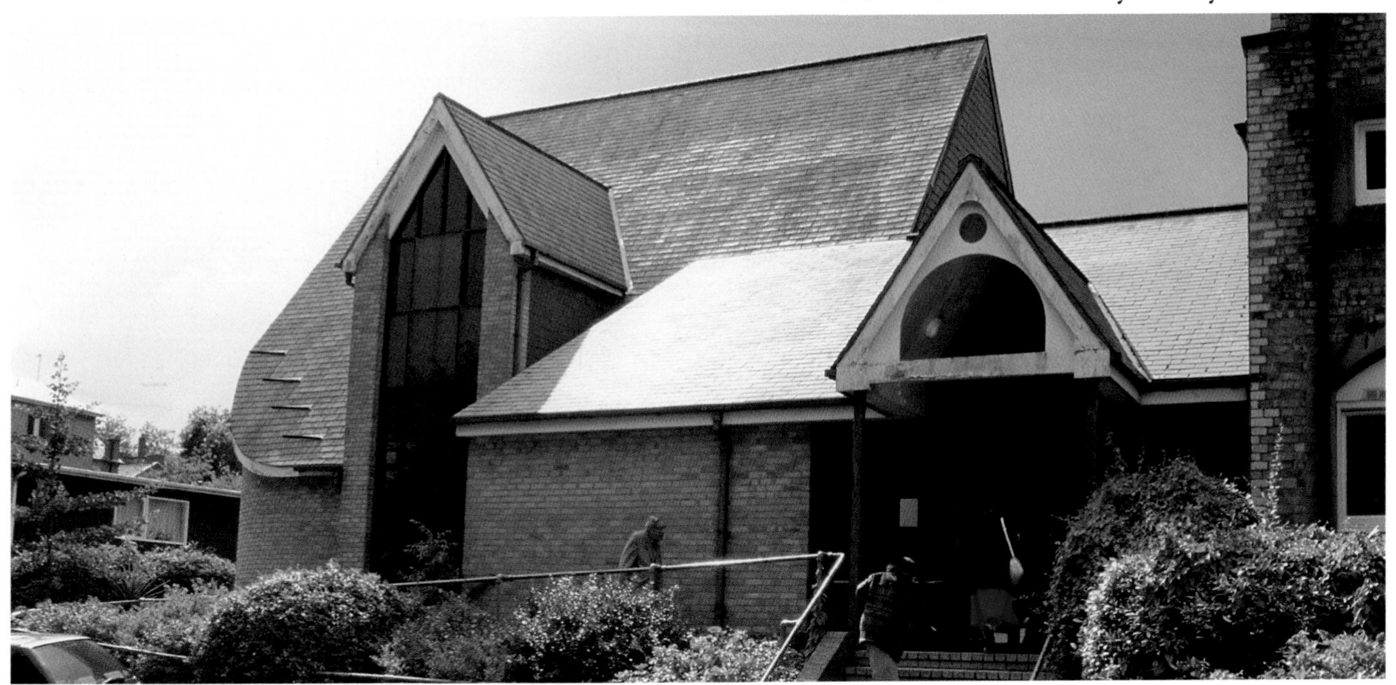

A large church

A traditional large church tells us much about the way many Christian buildings are designed for prayer.

Many Christian religious buildings are built on traditional lines, so let's look more closely at the main features of this kind of building.

In the shape of a cross

Picture (1) shows a typical shape for a large church. You can see that it has been built in the shape of a cross. This is because the cross is the most important symbol of Christianity.

Many churches are also built so that they point to the east. They are pointing towards the city of Jerusalem, in Israel, where Christianity began.

▲ (2) **This wooden SCREEN, called a rood screen, is sometimes used to separate the NAVE from the part of the church near the ALTAR.**

▼ (1) **The main features of a large church.**

Towers

On the outside of this church, you can see tall towers. Some churches have spires instead of towers. They help to give importance to the building. In past times, churches used to compete to have the tallest spire or tower.

The nave of this building is very long. There is room for a large **CONGREGATION** to sit there during worship. At the end of the nave farthest from the entrance is the chancel and the altar.

Inside the church

The largest space inside the church is called the **NAVE**. All of the arches inside this building help to support the roof. They also divide the nave into sections called aisles.

You can also see that the **CHANCEL**, the place where the choir sings, is beyond the nave. At the end of the chancel is the main **ALTAR**. The altar is always raised on a platform. This is so that people sitting in the nave look up at the altar (picture ②).

Running across the church, between the nave and the chancel is the transept. Some transepts also have an altar.

Places for private worship

Some parts of the church, often called **CHAPELS**, are used for small groups of people to worship together.

Tombs and statues

People who were important to the church, the country or the region are sometimes remembered through statues and tombs inside the church (picture ③).

▶ ③ **A statue on the tomb of an important person.**

Inside a church

The church is made of several parts.

When you go into a church you will see that it is really a large hall. This hall may or may not be divided into sections.

Nave

The **NAVE** is the main hall of a church, where the worshippers sit (picture ①). A large area is needed so that many people can worship together.

The nave may contain row after row of seats or benches (called **PEWS**) where people (called the **CONGREGATION**) can sit while they worship.

There may also be an organ, a large instrument that provides music for the service.

Near where you have entered the church there may be a **FONT** – a place where people are **BAPTISED** (see pages 12 and 13).

There will also be a high platform, called a **PULPIT**, where a preacher can stand while giving the **SERMON** (picture ②).

▼ ① **The nave starts at the back of the church and goes towards the altar. The pews in the nave always face towards the altar.**

▲ ② The pulpit is where the preacher stands when giving a sermon, or talk, during worship.

Chancel and altar

The entrance door for most churches is actually in the 'back' of the nave. So, when you walk inside the church, you look right along its length. You may find a **SCREEN** between the nave and the rest of the church. Beyond this is the chancel (picture ③), where the choir sits, and finally the altar.

▼ ③ The choir stalls are found between the nave and the altar in a part of the church called the chancel.

The altar and cross

The cross and the altar are the focus of a church.

The altar, with its cross, is the focus of the church.

The importance of the altar

The altar reminds worshippers of the table at which **JESUS CHRIST** and his **DISCIPLES** had their last meal together before Jesus was taken away and **CRUCIFIED**.

One way you can tell that the altar is very important is that all the pews face towards the altar. This is so that everyone can see the altar.

The altar is usually raised from the floor of the church and placed behind a railing called the altar rail.

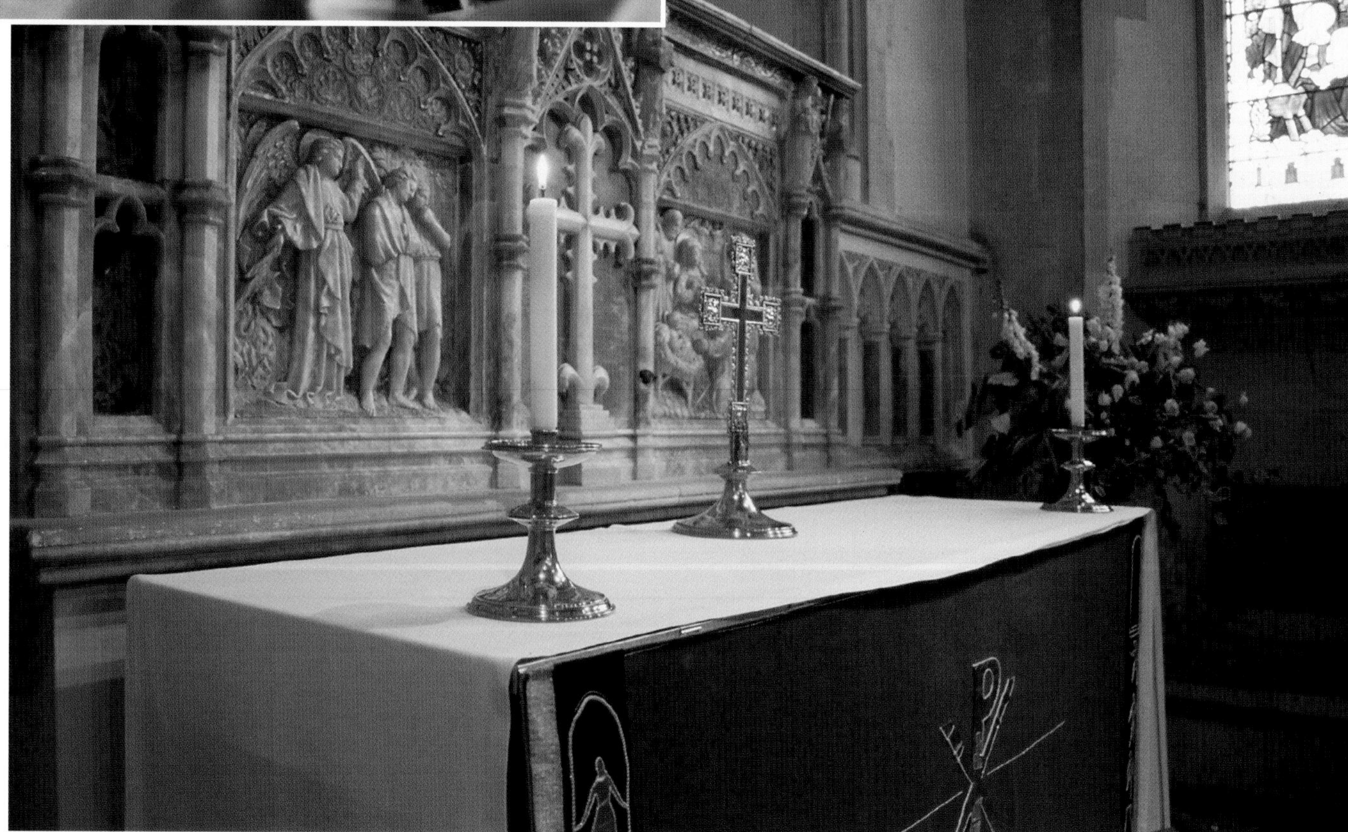

◄▼ (1) During worship an altar may contain a BIBLE, a cross, candles, a cup called the CHALICE and a special bread called the EUCHARIST. These pictures show you both traditional and modern altars.

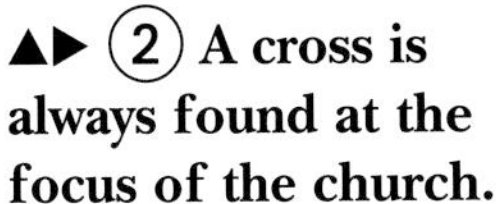

▲▶ ② A cross is always found at the focus of the church.

Behind and to the sides of the altar you may see windows, allowing the altar to be bathed in sunlight during the day (picture ①).

Behind the altar you may see a screen with paintings or carvings telling of events in the life of Jesus or the saints.

On the altar

If you were to ask people what was the most important part of a church, they would probably say the cross (picture ②).

The cross is the most important symbol of Christianity. It was on a cross that Jesus Christ died. Christians consider Him to be the sign of God. Jesus Christ is also called the saviour.

There are many crosses in a church, but the most important one is the one that is placed on the altar. The cross and altar together make the focus for worship in a church.

There are ceremonies called the **EUCHARIST**, **MASS**, **HOLY COMMUNION** or the **LORD'S SUPPER**. During these ceremonies bread and wine are placed on the altar. This reminds worshippers of the bread and wine that Jesus shared with his disciples during their last meal. The wine is held in a special cup called the **CHALICE**.

To be baptised

Christians are welcomed into the Christian community by being baptised. That is why the font is such an important part of the church.

When people are **BAPTISED** they are welcomed into the church. Christian families often have their children baptised when they are babies. This is the first step on the way to being confirmed as an adult member of the Christian church.

What is the font?

The **FONT** is the part of the church where Baptism takes place (picture ①). So, the font is therefore a very important part of the church.

The font is usually in the back of the nave, near the door that people use to enter the church. The font is placed here for an important reason. It reminds worshippers that when someone is baptised, they are entering the Christian religion.

The font can be any shape or size. Water is poured into it for the Baptism ceremony (picture ②).

Baptism as an adult

The first Christians were baptised, like Jesus, as adults. Some adults also want to be baptised. Many people feel that Baptism at this stage of life is like being born all over again. In fact, some Christians, for example, the Baptists, feel that it is important to put their whole body underwater during Baptism, and so their font is actually a small pool (picture ③). This kind of font is sometimes called a **BAPTISTRY**.

▲ ① People are baptised at the font. During Baptism, a member of the CLERGY says special blessings and then sprinkles some water from the font on to the person's head.

▲ ③ In some churches, people are baptised by putting their whole body underwater. In these churches, a very large font called a baptistry is used.

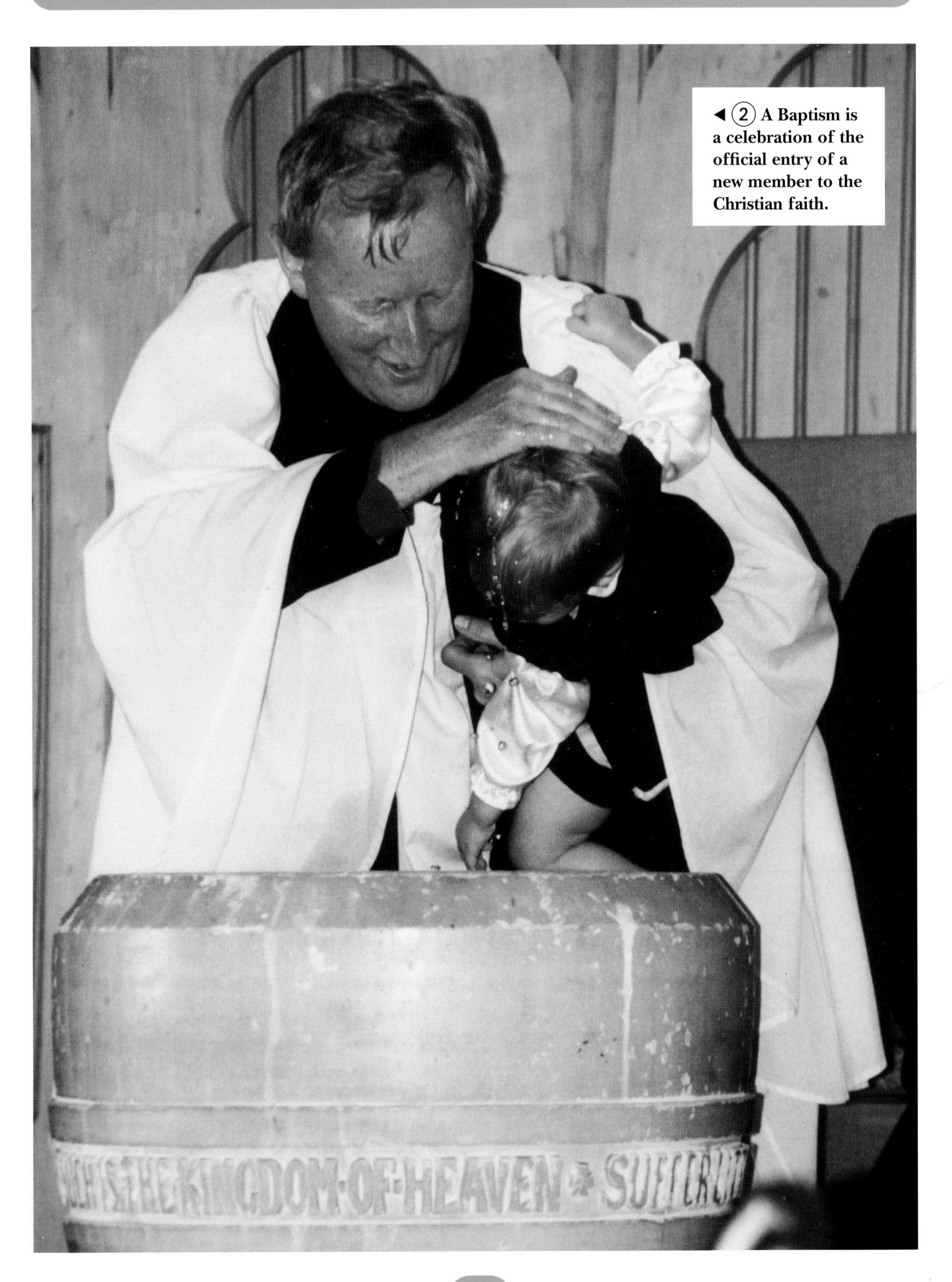

◀ (2) A Baptism is a celebration of the official entry of a new member to the Christian faith.

Different ways to worship

Some Christians find that items such as statues, candles and the confessional help them in their worship.

There are many different Christian religious groups in the UK. Two of the main groups are the Anglicans and the Roman Catholics. They worship in a similar way but there are some differences and these affect the arrangement of a church.

For example, in a Roman Catholic church, you may see a place near an altar or a statue where there are candles alight (picture ①). These are called **REMEMBRANCE CANDLES** or Votive candles. Worshippers light these candles in order to help them pray for living people or those who have died.

Special places

In almost all Roman Catholic churches there are tiny, curtained-off areas called **CONFESSIONALS**. Worshippers use these areas to speak or confess to God while a priest listens to them.

Roman Catholic and Anglican churches have a cupboard called

▼ ① These candles help people pray for their living friends and relatives and for those who are dead.

▲ ② Statues can also help people worship, by reminding them of important Christians and what they did. This is a statue of St Teresa of Liseaux, from a Roman Catholic church.

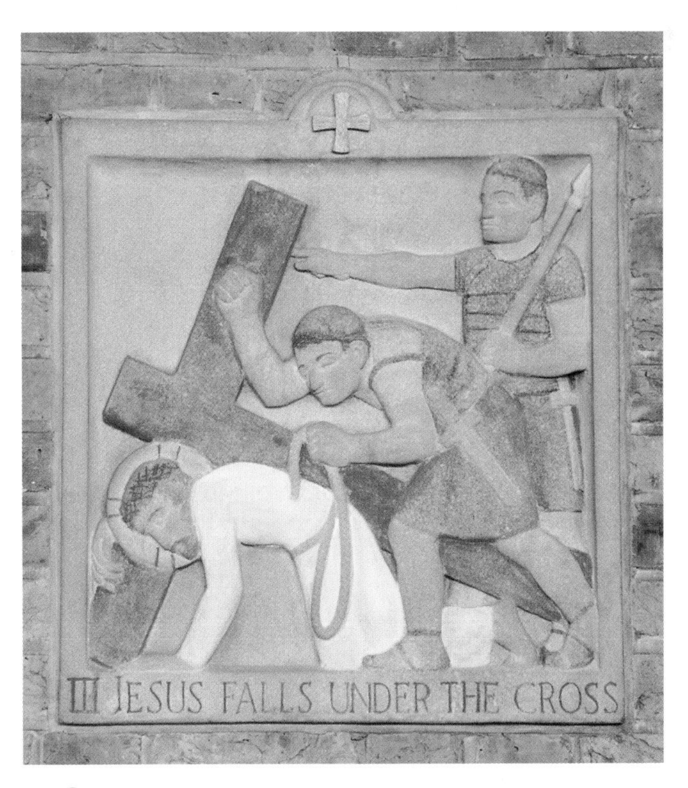

▲ ③ The stations of the cross are usually plaques or pictures that remind worshippers of 14 things that may have happened to Jesus on his way to be crucified. This is station three.

the **TABERNACLE**. Any bread and wine that is not used in the Eucharist is kept in the Tabernacle. This bread and wine may be taken to the homes of worshippers who are ill to perform the Eucharist there.

Statues help people pray

In some Roman Catholic and Anglican churches, people like to remember important Christians when they pray. To help them, these churches might have statues or paintings of, for example, important Christians from the past (picture ②).

Many Roman Catholic churches have statues of the **VIRGIN MARY**. These statues help remind worshippers about the life of the Virgin Mary and also help them to pray.

There might also be statues or paintings near the altar, where they can be used in worship.

Special objects that help people worship

As you look around a Roman Catholic and some Anglican churches, you may see 14 plaques or paintings on the walls. These are called the **STATIONS OF THE CROSS** (picture ③).

The stations of the cross remind worshippers of fourteen things that are believed to have happened to Jesus Christ on his way to be crucified.

Plain and simple buildings

Some people find it comforting to have a ceremony and a highly decorated building. Others find it enough to meet together in a simple room.

There are many different ways for Christians to express their faith. This is why churches do not all look the same inside or outside. For example, many churches do not have tall towers outside, or statues and paintings inside. Instead they look more like ordinary buildings.

Friends Meeting House

A church does not have to be a large building or even to have a large cross on the outside. Picture (1) shows a Friends Meeting House. There is no cross or **STAINED GLASS**. We know that it is a religious building because the sign in front tells us that it is used as a religious building.

In a Friends Meeting House the members of the meeting sit on benches or chairs arranged in a square, facing each other. There is no pulpit or font, and there are no statues. There is nothing on the inside or the outside of the building to distract worshippers from thinking about God.

▼ (1) This is a Friends Meeting House. You can only tell it is a religious building because of the sign at the front. The sign tells us that this is a Friends Meeting House, and tells us what time services are held.

Salvation Army Citadel

The Salvation Army Citadel is another place where people worship in plain surroundings (picture ②). However, there are more decorations than in a Friends Meeting House.

Instead of a cross, or a picture of Jesus Christ, there is a special Salvation Army emblem on the wall (picture ③).

There is no organ in a Salvation Army Citadel. Instead, there is a brass band (picture ④). The Salvation Army badge and the music of the brass band remind worshippers that they are part of God's "army".

▼ ③ Instead of a big cross, most Salvation Army churches have the Salvation Army emblem. The words "blood and fire" on the emblem remind worshippers that the church will help save them.

▼ ② The inside of a Salvation Army Citadel usually has few decorations. Worshippers sit on plain chairs and stand up to sing.

▲ ④ Most large Salvation Army Citadels have a brass band instead of an organ. The band wears a uniform. This reminds people that they are in an "army of God".

Stained glass

Many churches are decorated with stained glass windows. The windows are beautiful and the scenes in them help people worship.

When you walk into a church during the day, you might be amazed at all the beautiful colours coming from the windows. Windows like these, that are made from painted or coloured glass, are called **STAINED GLASS** windows (picture ①).

◄ ① **Stained glass windows like these play a part in worship in the church. The pictures on the windows help worshippers remember important stories from the Bible.**

▼ ② **Some stained glass windows show saints or important local people.**

Stained glass windows let light and colour into the church. Many churches have stained glass windows behind, and to the sides of the altar, so that it is bathed in colours. Some churches and **CATHEDRALS** have stained glass in almost every window.

Stained glass is very nice to look at, but it can also be helpful in worship.

Stories on windows

The stained glass windows in a church are often made so that they show scenes from the Bible or from Christian history (pictures ② and ③). The light shining through the stained glass makes the scenes look beautiful and bright.

A long time ago, when most people could not read, they would look at the stained glass windows to help them learn stories from the Bible. Today, most people can read, but stained glass windows are still used to remind people of important Christian stories and events.

▶ ③ Some churches have just a few, small, stained glass windows. But many large churches, and especially cathedrals, have stained glass in many windows. The stained glass cross in this Methodist church has pictures of the 12 disciples.

Cathedrals

A cathedral is the central or 'mother' church of an area called a diocese which is led by a bishop.

Of all the Christian buildings in the world, the ones that stand out the most are the cathedrals (pictures ① and ②).

What is a cathedral for?

The **CLERGY** in a **DIOCESE** work together. Their work is led by a bishop and a group of clergy who work at a cathedral. Important events for the city and churches of the diocese are held in the cathedral. There may be 'pop' style acts of worship or solemn ceremonies at the inauguration of a mayor and the **ORDINATION** of clergy. As in all churches there are regular services on Sundays and weekdays.

An awesome building

In the past, no money was spared to build the tallest and grandest cathedrals in honour of the glory of God. Many modern cathedrals follow the same tradition of having a large, awesome building. As a result, a cathedral is usually one of the largest and most awesome buildings in a city.

► ① Cathedrals like St Paul's, in London, are huge and awesome buildings.

Inside a cathedral

Just as a cathedral is built to look awesome on the outside, everything on the inside of a cathedral is also made to be huge and beautiful. For example, the nave of a cathedral might have room for thousands of people to sit (picture ③).

Inside the cathedral there might be artwork, stained glass windows (see pages 18 and 19), and a large, decorated altar and pulpit. All of these things make the cathedral a very special building.

◀ ② **Westminster Cathedral is a modern Roman Catholic cathedral.**

▲ ③ **The choir stalls at the end of the nave in St Paul's Cathedral.**

Special places inside the cathedral

A cathedral contains all the things that you find inside a church, such as the altar, font, pulpit and chapel. As in some churches, important people are buried in tombs or **CRYPTS** inside the cathedral. The tombs might be decorated with statues of the people buried there.

Cathedrals also have a special seat, called the bishop's throne. This is where the bishop of the diocese sits during worship.

Churches around the world

There are Christian religious buildings all around the world. These are often built using local materials and building styles.

Wherever people have built Christian buildings, they have often used the materials that were readily available. That is why many churches are built of stone. However, the church in picture ① is made from a kind of mud called adobe. Many buildings in desert areas of the world are made from adobe.

Different building styles

Churches also vary in shape and style from one part of the world to another. For example, in Ethiopia, Africa, some churches were carved out of rock in the shape of a cross (picture ②). By contrast, in Romania, Eastern Europe, some churches are of rounded shape and decorated with many paintings (picture ③) not just inside but also on all of the outside walls.

▼ ① This church, in the state of New Mexico in the USA, is made of mud. That is why it has to have very thick walls. In this area rainfall is uncommon, but nevertheless, the walls have to be repaired every year or so.

◀▲ ② An Ethiopian church in Lalibela. This church was carved out of rock and is sunk in the ground. You can see that it is in the shape of a cross.

▼ ③ A Romanian church, showing paintings on the inside (left) and outside (right) of the small countryside church.

Index

Curriculum Visions is a registered trademark of Atlantic Europe Publishing Company Ltd.

Atlantic Europe Publishing

Teacher's Guide
There is a Teacher's Guide to accompany this book, available only from the publisher.

Dedicated Web Site
There's more about other great Curriculum Visions packs and a wealth of supporting information available at our dedicated web site:

www.CurriculumVisions.com

First published in 2003 by Atlantic Europe Publishing Company Ltd

First reprint 2004. Second reprint 2006.

Authors
Lisa Magloff, MA and Brian Knapp, BSc, PhD
Religious Education Consultant
The Reverend Ian DH Robins, MA, BD, AKC
Art Director
Duncan McCrae, BSc
Editors
Barbara Bass, BA and Gillian Gatehouse
Senior Designer
Adele Humphries, BA
Acknowledgements
The publishers would like to thank the following for their help and advice: The vicar, verger and choir of St Nicholas church, Hurst; St James Church, Muswell Hill; Our Lady of Muswell Hill; Salvation Army; Muswell Hill Baptist Church; Friends Meeting House, Muswell Hill; the rector of Christ Church, Southborough.
Photographs
The Earthscape Picture Library except page 13: *Stella Wood.*
Illustrations
David Woodroffe
Designed and produced by
Earthscape Editions
Printed in China by
WKT Company Ltd

Christian church – *Curriculum Visions*
A CIP record for this book is available from the British Library
Paperback ISBN-10: 1 86214 751 5
Paperback ISBN-13: 978 1 86214 751 5
Hardback ISBN: 1 86214 308 0

This product is manufactured from sustainable managed forests. For every tree cut down at least one more is planted.

Contents

Some words are shown in bold, **like this**. You can find out what they mean by looking in the glossary.

Light and dark

Look around the room you are in. What can you see? Imagine you are looking at the same room when it is completely dark. What would you see then? The room would stay the same and everything would stay where it is – but you would not be able to see in the dark. You can only see the objects in the room when there is light. Darkness is what you get when there is no light.

We can see clearly in the light, but when it gets darker we cannot see things as well.

EXPLORING LIGHT

Louise and Richard
Spilsbury

Raintree is an imprint of Capstone Global Library Limited, a company incorporated in England and Wales having its registered office at 264 Banbury Road, Oxford OX2 7DY – Registered company number: 6695582

www.raintree.co.uk
myorders@raintree.co.uk

Edited by Penny West
Designed by Rich Parker
Original illustrations © Capstone Global Library Ltd 2015
Illustrated by HL Studios
Picture research by Tracy Cummins
Production by Helen McCreath
Originated by Capstone Global Library Ltd
Printed and bound in China by CTPS

ISBN 978 1 406 29908 3 (hardback)
19 18 17 16 15
10 9 8 7 6 5 4 3 2 1

ISBN 978 1 406 29913 7 (paperback)
20 19 18 17 16
10 9 8 7 6 5 4 3 2 1

Spilsbury, Louise and Richard
Light and Dark (Exploring Light)

British Library Cataloguing in Publication Data
A full catalogue record for this book is available from the British Library.

Acknowledgements
We would like to thank the following for permission to reproduce photographs:
Capstone Press: HL Studios, 7, 18, Karon Dubke, 8, 9, 12, 13, 16, 17, 20, 21, 24, 25, 28, 29; iStockphoto: RapidEye, 10, SoumenNath, 11; Shutterstock: agsandrew, Design Element, Alexander Ishchenko, 6, ALMAGAMI, Design Element, Christopher Wood, 23, Click Bestsellers, Design Element, Dennis Tokarzewski, Design Element, EML, 5, GaudiLab, 22, ID1974, Design Element, Ivan_Sabo, 19, kurt, Cover, l i g h t p o e t, 27, luckypic, Design Element, Michelangelus, 14, Ryan M. Bolton, 26, Smit, 15, Vadim Petrakov, 4, Vass Zoltan, Design Element.

We would like to thank Catherine Jones for her invaluable help in the preparation of this book.

Light helps us to see in the dark and keeps us safe at night. The flashing lights on a fire engine warn us to get out of its way. Traffic lights tell drivers when to stop and go. The lights on a lighthouse keep ships from crashing into dangerous rocks along the shore.

Close your eyes.

This is what it is like in a really dark place. How would you find your way around in the dark if you did not have a light?

Lights help to keep us safe. Red lights tell drivers to stop at crossings. A green light in the shape of a person tells people when it is safe to cross.

Light and sight

We cannot see in the dark because we need light for sight. We see some objects because they give off their own light. Stars, light bulbs, candles and other things that give out light of their own are called **light sources**. We see light sources because the light they make comes directly to our eyes. Most of the things we see, such as books, balls, grass and people, are not light sources, so how can we see them?

We see some things, such as fires, when it is dark because they give off their own light.

We see most objects when light shines on them and bounces back to our eyes. When light bounces off something we say it is **reflected**. Light reflects off surfaces rather like a ball bounces off the ground. For example, other people can only see you when light bounces off your surface and reflects light to their eyes!

The Sun

The Sun is our most important source of light. During the day, its light reflects off objects all around us to light up our world.

When light from a torch bounces off a path and other surfaces around it, we see where we are going because some of that reflected light enters our eyes.

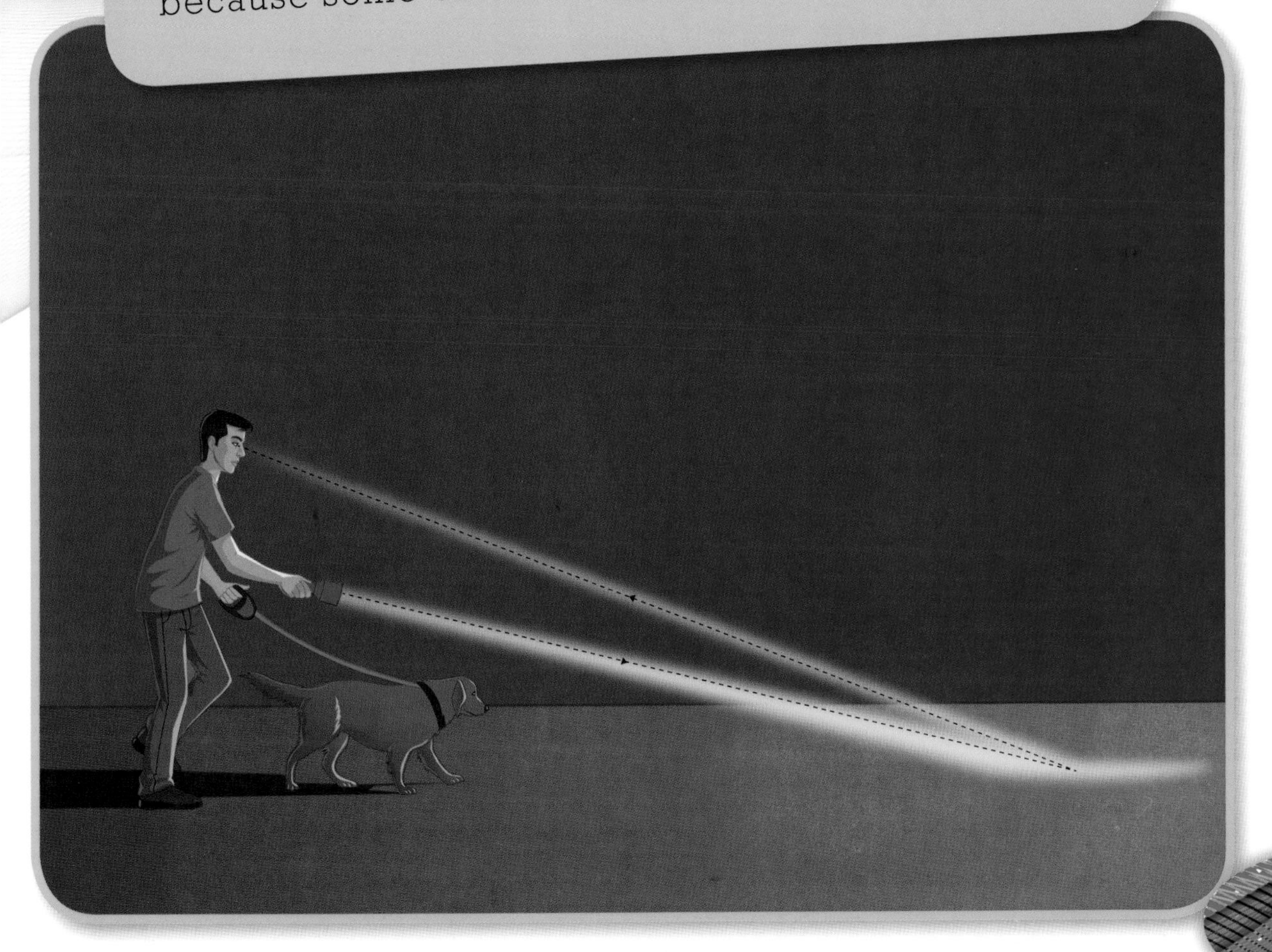

Activity: Make a dark box

How do we see in the dark?
Make a dark box to find out.

What you need

- a large box with a lid
- black paper
- sticky tape
- scissors
- a thin nail
- small objects such as a ball, a pencil and a coin
- a small torch.

What to do

1 Take off the lid and cut pieces of black paper to fit all over the inside of the box. Stick them on with the sticky tape. When you put the lid on, this will make a completely dark, black box.

2 Ask an adult to help you use the nail to make a small hole in one of the short ends of the box.

3 Put an object at the back of the box, opposite your peephole. Put the lid on the box.

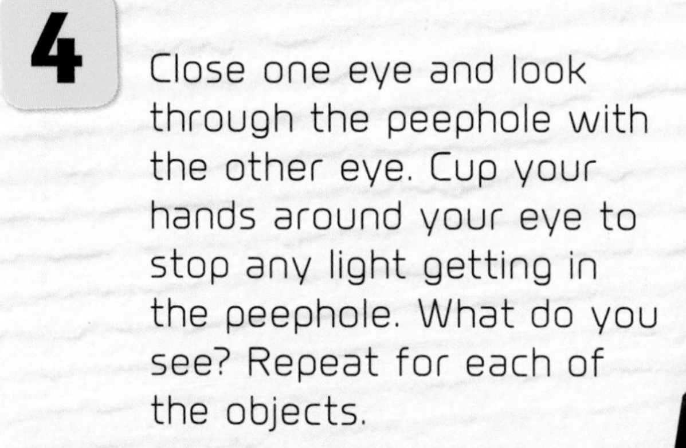

4 Close one eye and look through the peephole with the other eye. Cup your hands around your eye to stop any light getting in the peephole. What do you see? Repeat for each of the objects.

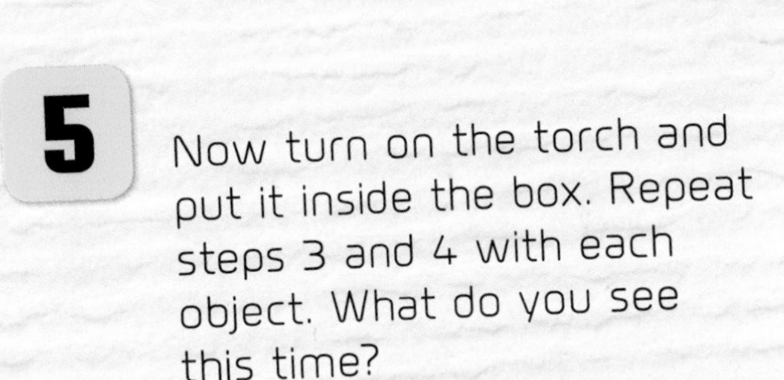

5 Now turn on the torch and put it inside the box. Repeat steps 3 and 4 with each object. What do you see this time?

What happens?

When you look into the dark box without the torch, you shouldn't be able to see anything because it is completely dark inside. When you look into the dark box when the torch is on, you should be able to see all the objects because light **reflects** off them. We need light to travel to our eyes to be able to see. Light from the torch hits the objects and bounces back (is reflected) to your eye.

Brighter and dimmer

To read a book at night we turn on a bright lamp. In restaurants people often use candles to give a soft light. Some **light sources** are brighter than others because they release more **energy**. Energy is the power that makes things work or move. A candle flame has a small amount of energy so it only lights up a small area around itself. A big ceiling light that is powered by **electricity** releases enough light energy to light up a whole room.

A candle gives out a dim light that only lights the darkness immediately around itself.

Diwali is the festival of lights. Diwali candles would be barely visible in daylight but twinkle brightly in the dark.

Lights look brighter when they are closer to us. That is why it gets darker as you move away from a light source. Lights appear brightest when it is dark all around them. If you turn on a torch in daylight you will barely see its light, but at night torchlight seems very bright.

Star light, star bright

Have you ever wondered why some stars look brighter than others? A star's brightness depends on how far away it is from Earth and the amount of light energy it gives off.

Activity: Testing lights

Test how distance affects the brightness of an object.

What you need

- chalk
- a tape measure
- two identical torches with new batteries
- two friends or helpers, including one adult.

What to do

1 Find a large room or space such as a hall that you can make dark. Make a chalk mark at one end to mark the starting point. Use the tape measure to measure two distances from this point, one at 3 metres (about 10 feet) and another at 9 metres (about 30 feet). Mark these distances with your chalk, too.

2 Close any curtains and turn off the lights to make the room dark. Stand beside the starting point mark. Ask your helpers to take the torches and stand side by side next to the second chalk mark, 3 metres (about 10 feet) away. They should turn on their lights and shine them towards you. Look at the lights for just a moment. Compare the brightness of the two lights.

3 Ask one of the helpers to walk back to the third chalk mark, 9 metres (about 30 feet) away, shining the light towards you all the time. When they stop, compare the brightness of the lights again.

4 Now ask the second helper to do the same. How does the brightness of the lights compare now?

What happens?

When your helpers both stand 3 metres (about 10 feet) away from you, the lights look equally bright. When one moves further away, the closer light looks brighter. When they both move to the 9-metre (30-foot) marker, they both appear dimmer than they did from the 3-metre (10-foot) marker. One of the reasons a light could be brighter than another is that it is closer to us.

Day and night

Why is it light during the day and dark at night? The reason is that Earth is like a giant ball that **rotates** or spins. Every 24 hours it turns round completely. This means that when one half of Earth is facing the Sun, the other is turned away from it. The half facing the Sun is in the light, so has daytime. The half facing away from the Sun is in darkness and has night.

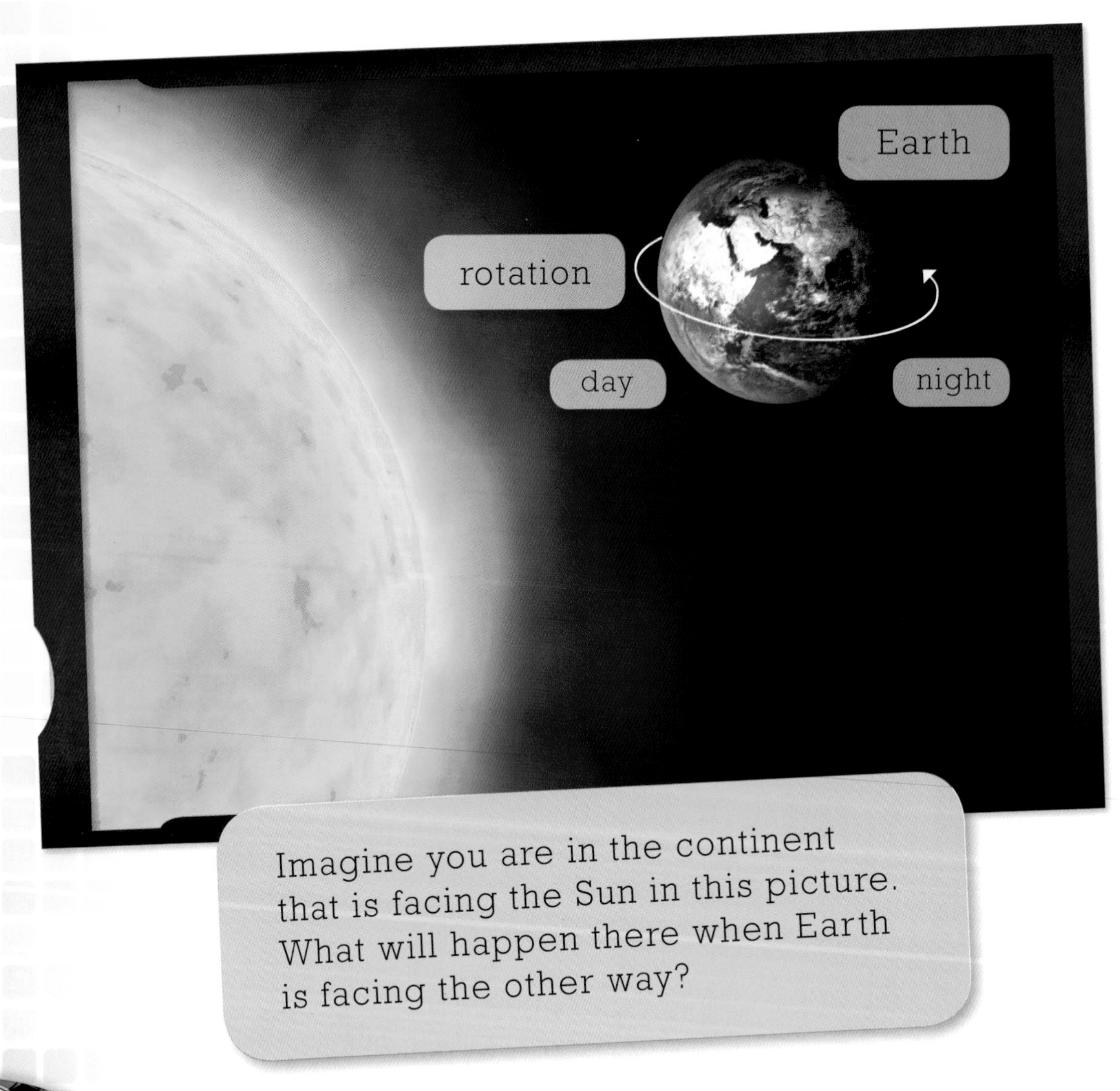

Imagine you are in the continent that is facing the Sun in this picture. What will happen there when Earth is facing the other way?

It is not always dark at night. Sometimes the Moon glows and gives off a soft light in the darkness. But the Moon is not a **light source**. Moonlight is just sunlight that **reflects** off the surface of the Moon!

Disappearing stars?

The stars are in the sky day and night. During the day the Sun makes the sky so bright that we cannot see the other, dimmer stars. At night, the Sun's rays are blocked by the other side of Earth, so we can see the faint light of the stars twinkling in space.

Activity: Making day and night

In this activity your head becomes planet Earth and experiences day and night, dark and light!

What you need

- a dark room
- a lamp with a lampshade.

What to do

1 Ask an adult to help you remove the lampshade. Turn on the lamp. The light bulb that shines in all directions represents the Sun.

2 Face the lamp and hold your hands either side of your face, with the palms facing forwards. Your head represents planet Earth. Imagine the North Pole is at the top of your head! Your hands mark the points east and west.

3 If your head were planet Earth, what time of day do you think it would be for a person located at your nose? Where would the Sun be in the sky?

4 Now, standing on the same spot, slowly turn a quarter way round to the right. What time of the day do you think it would be at your nose now? Turn a quarter way round again so your back is to the lamp. What time of day is it at your nose now? Turn another quarter. What is the time of day now?

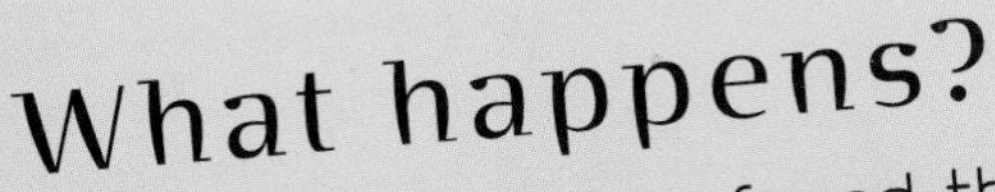

What happens?

At first, when you faced the lamp (Sun) directly, your nose would have been in full, direct sunlight and if your head really were Earth, it would have been noon or midday around your nose. As you turned, your nose would have been at different times of the day: sunset, night, sunrise and then back to midday!

Colours of light

The sunlight that lights up our world during the day is called white light, but sunlight is not just one colour. It is made up of different colours mixed together. When sunlight **reflects** off different objects, some of its colours are reflected and some are **absorbed** (soaked up). This is how we see different colours.

When sunlight shines on a red apple, most of the colours are absorbed. The red part of the sunlight reflects off the apple, so we see the apple as red.

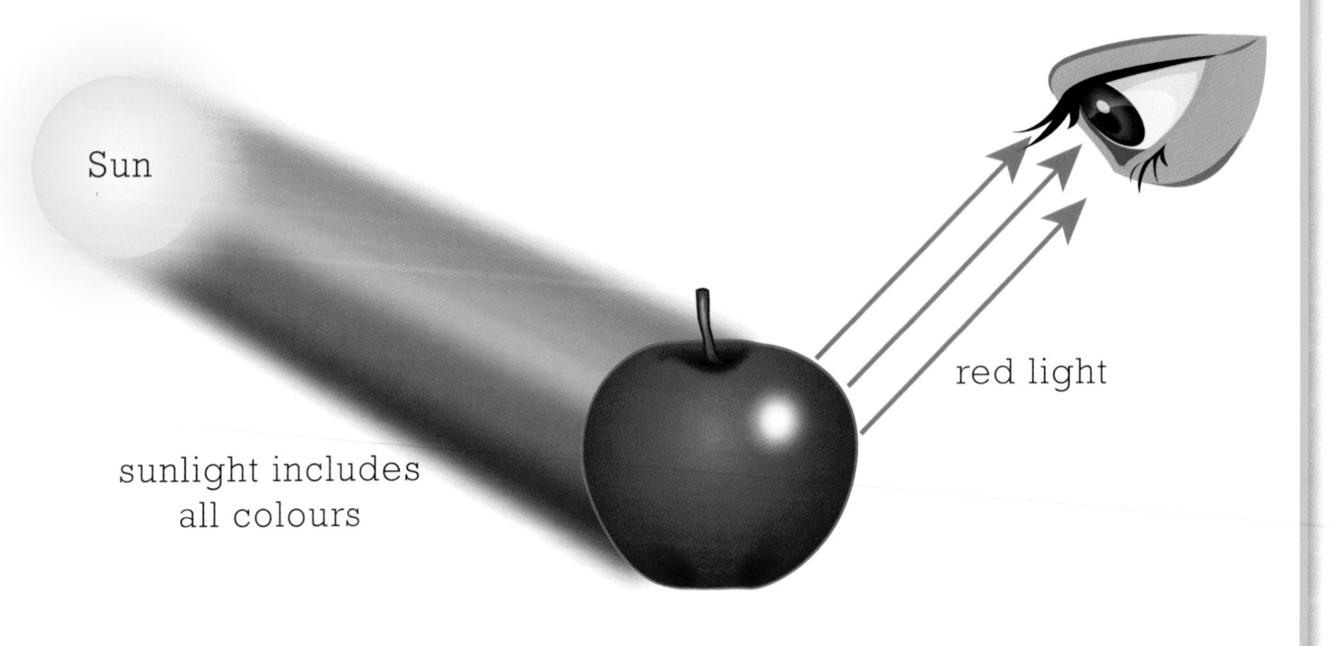

We can see all of the different colours in sunlight when there is a rainbow. Rainbows usually happen after rain when the air is full of tiny water drops. As sunlight passes through the droplets, the different colours are separated so that you can see them. Have you ever seen anything else that can make a rainbow? You may have seen a crystal or an oily puddle reflecting light. The white light is split into the different colours. How many different colours are there?

A rainbow happens when sunlight is split into its different colours.

Activity: Make a rainbow

You can split white light into its colours to make a rainbow of your own!

What you need

- a shallow pan, such as a baking tray
- water
- a small mirror
- Blutac or modelling clay
- a torch
- a white surface or white card.

What to do

1 Fill the shallow pan about halfway with water.

2 Lean the mirror at one end of the tray, at an **angle**. You might need some Blutac or modelling clay to hold it in place.

3 Ask a friend to use the torch to shine light at the part of the mirror that is under water.

4 Hold the white card above the mirror. Keep changing the angle at which it faces the mirror until you see a rainbow on the white card.

What happens?

When you shine the torch at the part of the mirror that is under water, the water splits the white light into all the different colours and a rainbow appears.

Dark and light surfaces

Which colour clothes do you usually wear on a hot, sunny day? Would you choose a light-coloured shirt or a dark one? Most people wear lighter-coloured clothing in summer because this helps them to stay cooler. Lighter-coloured surfaces **reflect** more light than darker ones. Dark-coloured surfaces **absorb** much more light and some of this light **energy** is released as warmth. When your shirt warms up, you get hotter, too!

Wearing tight, dark-coloured clothing during the summer can make you feel hotter.

The white surfaces of the Arctic help to keep the area cold by reflecting away light energy that would turn to heat if absorbed.

Black and white colours are the best colours for keeping warm or keeping cool. A black surface is one that does not reflect any light. It is black because all of the colours of light are absorbed. As black absorbs the most energy, black surfaces also release most heat. White surfaces reflect all colours.

Arctic ice and snow

One of the reasons it is freezing cold at the Arctic is all the ice and snow there. These pure white surfaces reflect around 90 per cent of the sunlight that hits them back into the air. Ocean water only reflects 10 per cent.

Activity: Light and heat

Test whether the colour of a material affects how much heat it **absorbs**.

What you need

- black paper
- white paper (the same type and size as the black paper)
- two identical drinking glasses or jars
- two elastic bands or sticky tape
- a measuring jug
- water
- a sunny day
- a thermometer.

What to do

1 Wrap the black paper around one of the glasses using an elastic band or sticky tape to hold it on. Do the same with the white paper and the other glass.

2 Use the measuring jug to make sure you fill both glasses with exactly the same amount of water from a cold tap. Leave the glasses outside in the sunshine in a safe place such as on a table.

3 After a couple of hours use the thermometer to measure the temperature of the water in each glass. What do you notice?

What happens?

Dark surfaces, such as the black paper, absorb more light than lighter ones, such as white paper. The light that is absorbed turns to heat. You should find that the temperature of the water in the glass with the black paper around it is hotter than the one with white paper around it. This is because lighter surfaces **reflect** more light and so stay cooler.

Animals in the dark

We need light to find our way in the dark, but some animals have eyes that allow them to see at night. Many **nocturnal** animals have large eyes to collect more light. This helps them see in dim light. An owl's eyes fill over one half of its head and each one of a tarsier's eyes is the same size and weight as its brain!

The tarsier has the biggest eyes of any **mammal** compared to its head size.

A hare's large ears are constantly twitching to help detect and hear small sounds.

Some nocturnal animals use hearing and other senses to find things when it is too dark to see. Cats have ears that turn and twist to help them hear exactly where a sound is coming from. Rabbits and hares have long ears to help them hear foxes and other animals that try to eat them. Some nocturnal animals have a strong sense of smell. A fox's large ears hear well and its long nose helps it to sniff out **prey**.

Cats' eyes

At the back of a cat's eye there is a special layer that **reflects** light and doubles the amount of light they can use. When you see a cat's eyes glowing at night, you are really seeing the reflected light.

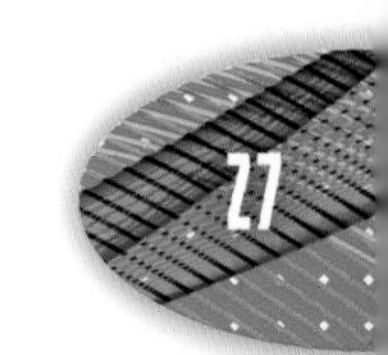

Activity: Super senses

Try this test to find out how our sense of hearing can help us "see" in the dark.

What you need

- a friend
- a chair
- a blindfold
- a selection of items that make noise, such as coins, a book, a newspaper, a ball, paper, aluminium foil, a stapler, a bottle of fizzy drink
- a pen and paper.

What to do

1. Sit your friend on a chair with the blindfold on.

2. Stand about a metre (3 feet) away and make noises with your different items. Bounce the ball, crumple the foil, undo the bottle of fizzy drink, close the stapler. Can your friend guess what is making each noise? Write down their answers.

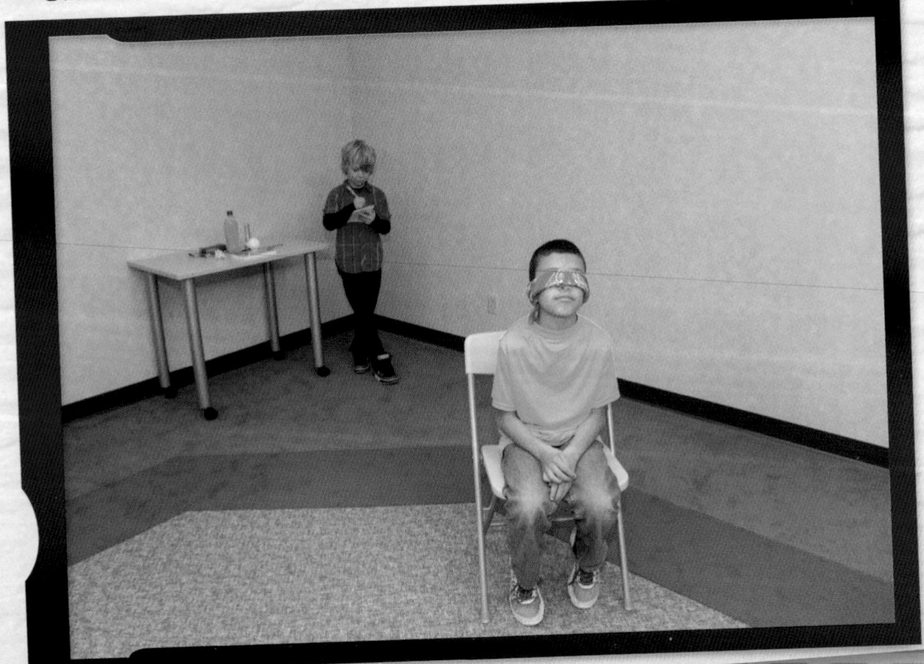

3

Ask your friend to cover their ears while you move to a different spot further away. Make a noise again. Can they point to exactly where you are standing? Move again and ask them to point to where you are again.

What happens?

Your friend probably got a lot of answers right. When our eyes are closed and we concentrate, we can use our sense of hearing to tell us a lot about what is around us.

You should also find that the blindfolded person can point to where you are quite accurately when you make a noise. Our two ears help us judge direction and distance. The ear closest to the sound hears it a little louder and slightly sooner than the other ear.

Glossary

absorb to soak up or take in something

angle amount or measure of a turn between two straight lines that meet at one end

electricity type of energy we usually use to make machines work

energy the power that makes things work or move

light source something that makes or gives off light, such as the Sun or a torch

mammal animal that usually has some hair on its body and gives birth to live young that feeds on milk from its mother's body

nocturnal to be active at night

prey animal that is hunted and eaten by another animal

reflect to bounce back light off a surface

rotate to turn in circles around a central point. Car wheels, merry-go-rounds and spinning tops all rotate.

Find out more

Books

Glaring Light and Other Eye-burning Rays (Disgusting and Dreadful Science), Anna Claybourne (Franklin Watts, 2013)

Light (Amazing Science), Sally Hewitt (Wayland, 2014)

Light and Colour (Straight Forward with Science), Peter Riley (Franklin Watts, 2015)

Light and Dark (Light All Around Us), Daniel Nunn (Raintree, 2012)

Websites

www.bbc.co.uk/learningzone/clips/day-and-night-on-earth/1874.html

On this BBC website the animation shows you how we get night and day on Earth.

www.bbc.co.uk/schools/scienceclips/ages/5_6/light_dark.shtml

You can investigate light and dark on this BBC website.

www.childrensuniversity.manchester.ac.uk/interactives/science/earthandbeyond/shadows

Find out more about how day and night happen on this University of Manchester website.

www.glasgowsciencecentre.org/online/dark-and-light-day-and-night.html

Join Jack and Alice as they explore the concepts of dark and light in an animated story on the Glasgow Science Centre website.

Index